S t u d y   G

THIRSTING FOR GOD

A Spiritual Journey Towards
Restoration and Renewal

N I C H O L A S   K I N G

kevin
mayhew

First published in 2003 by
KEVIN MAYHEW LTD
Buxhall, Stowmarket, Suffolk, IP14 3BW
E-mail: info@kevinmayhewltd.com
KINGSGATE PUBLISHING INC
1000 Pannell Street, Suite G, Columbia, MO 65201
E-mail: sales@kingsgatepublishing.com

9 8 7 6 5 4 3 2 1 0
ISBN 1 84417 169 8
Catalogue No. 1500653

Cover design by Angela Selfe
Typesetting by Simon Loxley
Printed and bound in Great Britain

CONTENTS

Introduction

The theme of this short book, 'thirsting for God', originated in a very dark time in my life when, although I was already an ordained priest, I had gone into what seemed dreadfully like atheism. This meant that I felt like a terrible hypocrite every time I presided at a service, and wondered if I should not abandon the pretence and get married and 'do something useful'. For reasons which I cannot explain now, except in terms of the leading of that impossibly distant God, I kept at it, and continued to pray and do everything else, just as though it were all true. And, eventually, it came back, though in a different and unexpected way, with a deeper understanding of the mystery of our dark God. One stage in this process I shall never forget. While I was still in the darkness, I was in a chapel in Guyana, South America, and a ray of light fell on an altar-cloth, just where a text from Psalm 42 was embroidered in Latin: 'My soul thirsts for you, O God'. It was not the end of my darkness, but suddenly I realised that it was true – all that time I had simply been longing for God (and, of course, that longing buried deep in all of us, carries with it an assurance that ultimately it will be fulfilled).

Later reflection, and further experience as a priest, made me realise that every human being has this thirst, because we are made in God's image and likeness. Obviously, we do not all recognise this thirst, and we try all manner of things that might slake it; but it is there, and this book offers some meditations to enable you to engage with your thirst – to recognise it, and quench it in God, who alone can satisfy us. This book is aimed particularly at those who find themselves walking in that frightening darkness where there seems to be no God and no purpose to life.

The format is a simple one, and you must use it as you feel best. Each chapter has an introduction, to set the scene, then an anecdote from my life or that of others close to me, and some texts from the New Testament which I have translated afresh, in order to try and bring out their raw power. The translation consciously tries to keep close to the original Greek. In particular, I have tried not to smooth over the roughnesses and oddities of the original. Translation, especially of much-loved texts, is not just difficult: it is impossible. Therefore it is quite likely that tomorrow I shall translate a given passage quite differently from how I have translated it today. If it encourages you to go back to your favourite translation of the New Testament (or, better still, to several different versions), that will be all to the good. Nothing in this book depends on particular translations; all depends on your encounter with the God who waits just below the surface of the text. Read the texts through as though for the first time, not as an exercise in piety, but as a way of encountering what lies deepest within you. What matters in this book is what goes on, as you read and reflect and pray, between you and the mystery to which we give the deceptively easy name of 'God'. At the beginning and end of each chapter is a prayer, intended to set the mood. Use it only if you find it helpful. Each chapter concludes with three questions to focus your thoughts before the final prayer, whether you are reading as an individual or as part of a group.

The book has seven chapters, and some people might like to use it for the six-and-a-half weeks of Lent that lead up to Easter, the greatest Christian feast. Use it as you will, however, and if just one reader is brought into contact with their deepest thirst, then the work will have been justified.

There are a good many footnotes in the translations, which can give the text an uncomfortably 'speckled' appearance. They are not there to alarm you, nor to impress (or depress) you with a demonstration of great learning, but to help you to get the 'feel' of some of the texts, what it might have been like to read or, more likely, to hear them the first time. They are intended to encourage readers to look more closely at the text than perhaps they usually do; and they should also serve to stimulate group discussion, or individual reflection, on various points.

A good deal of the material offered in these reflections has its origin in talks given at various times to the National Retreat Movement in Southport, England, to the priests of the diocese of Fort Worth in Texas, and to the monks of Douai Abbey in England; I am grateful to all of these for their feedback and suggestions.

Thanks are due also to my Jesuit brethren, Frs Gerry J. Hughes and Philip Endean, who helpfully read through some or all of various drafts of this book, and who greatly improved it with their suggestions. The book and its author owe an enormous debt to its copy editor, Revd Peter Dainty, who was splendidly sharp-eyed with my sloppiness and firm in demanding consistency. His work has enabled the book's message to come across far more clearly than it would have done otherwise.

Nicholas King SJ

Dedication

This book is dedicated in gratitude to two families who
have taught me so much of my thirst for God: the family I was
born into (my parents, sister and brothers and their extended
families), who planted that thirst in me, and the family of the
Society of Jesus, who nurtured it.

Nicholas King was educated at Stonyhurst in Lancashire
and St John's College, Oxford. He joined the Jesuits in
1970, and has taught in schools, seminaries and universities.
He taught New Testament studies in South Africa
for many years, and is currently Spiritual Father and Tutor
in New Testament at Campion Hall, Oxford.
He has written a number of books and articles, and frequently
lectures on New Testament subjects to a wide range of audiences.
He is currently working on a new and radically fresh translation
from the Greek of the New Testament.

CHAPTER 1

Identifying the Thirst Correctly

Opening Prayer

God our Loving Father,
we know that we are thirsty;
but we do not always know what we are thirsty for.
Give us the grace to know our deepest desires
and to find their fulfilment in you. Amen.

Everyone Has the Same Thirst

We need to beware the easy assumption that those who do not go to church, or those who do not share our values or lifestyle, are not open to the transcendent God. What follows is built on the assumption that every human being has inside them a thirst, given by God, which only God can slake. They do not always identify it correctly, but the thirst is there.

John's story

John (we shall call him that) was a pious boy at school, almost unusually so, but something went wrong. When he had just left school he was, as he described it to me, 'raped, if such a thing is possible, by an older woman', and that started a fairly rapid slide towards the dogs, complicated by difficult times when on active service in the armed forces. He tried the kind of things that people ordinarily try under such circumstances, including drink, almost to the point of alcoholism, drugs, cigarettes, and sex. He fathered two children, and procured their abortion, lost contact with his family, with himself, and with God. But people were praying for him and, slightly to his surprise, he found himself one day in a well-known place of pilgrimage and confessing his regrets and hurts and being reconciled to God. His story since has been one of finding God, and of constantly deepening prayer, all in the context of a successful job and a very happy marriage. Now he can see where his thirst will be slaked.

We all have this thirst for God; we do not, however, always know what to do with the thirst. Sometimes we try to slake it in whatever way we can. You know the list of 'usual suspects': sex, drugs, alcohol, gambling, violence, religion. There are, however, plenty of other ways in which we defend ourselves against the demands of God: by seeking status or fame or power or by nursing resentments. And there are all those moments of unobtrusive selfishness that no one notices (or so we think).

If these various stratagems are not steps taken in the direction of God, in the service of God, then they will not slake our thirst, will not leave us content. So every action we take, every decision we make, must (if we are to find the happiness that each of us is looking for) lead us towards the God for whom we long, and not in any other direction.

Look now at this first of our New Testament texts, the story of one I have called the 'bumptious pietist'. (You may have other names for him.) Read these New Testament texts through several times, let them work on your imagination, and let your imagination work on them. Above all, listen for the voice of God. That voice may come as a challenge or as an invitation, as encouragement for your faltering steps or as deflation for complacency. Whatever you do, accept no substitute for the real thing, for nothing else will quench the thirst for God that is the deepest part of you.

A *bumptious pietist (Mark 10:17-22)*

> And as he was journeying on to [the] road, one running up and falling on his knees to him[1] said, 'Good teacher, what shall I do that I may inherit eternal life?'
>
> But Jesus said to him, 'Why do you call me good?[2] No one is good except the one God. You know the commandments: thou shalt not kill; thou shalt not commit adultery; thou shalt not steal; thou shalt not bear false witness; thou shalt not defraud; honour thy father and thy mother.'[3]
>
> But he said to him, 'Teacher, all these things I have kept from my youth.'[4]
>
> But Jesus looked at him and loved him and said to him, 'One thing you lack. Go, [and] sell whatever you have and give to the poor and you will have treasure in heaven and, come here, follow me.'
>
> But he was appalled at the suggestion, and went off grieving. For he had many possessions.

The bumptious pietist had a thirst, but he did not know the shape of it, and thought that it could not be slaked if he let go of his possessions. Jesus could only bring this home to him by his extraordinarily unwelcoming response. It was not that Jesus did not want him as a disciple, for he 'looked at him and loved him'. It was simply that without addressing the question of what he was *really* thirsting for, our bumptious pietist (who is certainly us, at least in certain of our moods) could not find his way to quench that thirst in Jesus, and in the God whom Jesus called 'Abba'.

Consider this story's setting in Mark's Gospel. Immediately before it, children are brought to Jesus for him to touch – to the consternation of the disciples (10:13), and to bless (10:16). Children are quite

---

1 The awkwardness here is in Mark, and has been deliberately preserved in the translation.

2 There is considerable shock here: the reader is supposed to ask, 'But surely Jesus *is* good?'

3 Which commandments are omitted? Which has been inserted? What does this tell us about the pietist's 'thirst'?

4 In which case the pietist deserves a round of stunned applause.

unselfconscious about their thirst, and, very often, quite unselfconscious about their need for God as well; they have much to teach us who think ourselves too grown-up to be bothered with our thirst for God. See also what follows the story of 'the bumptious pietist': the teaching that possessions stand in the way of slaking the thirst (10:22-27), and the certainty that letting go 'for my sake, and for the sake of the gospel' ensures quenching the thirst a hundred times over in the here and now (as well as persecutions). There is nothing easy about following the Lord; but once we have grasped what is really on offer, nothing will hold us back from it.

Moral dwarfs and moral giants (Luke 23:6-12)

Pilate, hearing [the mention of Galilee] asked if the fellow was Galilean. When he found that he was from Herod's[1] jurisdiction, he sent him up to Herod, who was in Jerusalem at the time. When Herod saw Jesus, he was delighted; because he had been anxious to see him for a long time, having heard about him. He was hoping to see some miracle being done by him. He interrogated him at some length; but [Jesus] made absolutely no reply to him. The Chief Priests and Scribes stood [there], vehemently accusing him.

But Herod thought him insignificant, and with his troops he made fun of him. They put a splendid robe on him and sent him up to Pilate. Herod and Pilate became friends on that day. For they had been at enmity before.

The contrast between Jesus and the 'bumptious pietist' is that Jesus did not accept the plausible persuasions about how to slake his thirst; only God would do for him, whereas the bumptious one wanted 'God *and* possessions', and that package simply is not on offer, nor will it quench our thirst. Jesus, like all human beings,

---

1 Not Herod the Great, who attempted to butcher Jesus at birth, but his son Herod Antipas, who had inherited part of his father's kingdom, and all of his unpleasantness.

grows to his full moral height by his absolute refusal to compromise with God's values. Look at the above story from Luke's account of Jesus' passion, and the unholy alliance between Pilate and Herod. These two are the top men of the area respectively: the Roman Emperor's principal representative in Judea, and the local princeling who held sway in Galilee. Set them against Jesus, and see how Jesus' awareness of where his thirst is quenched contrasts with their desperate clinging to power and authority.

Jesus says absolutely nothing here. But see how he towers above the rest: Pilate, looking for a way out of an awkward situation ('a Galilean? – send him to Herod!'); Herod, wanting a bit of excitement, but finding only frustration and disappointment, his enthusiasm turning to contempt and mockery (for the background, see Luke 3:19-20, 9:9, 13:31); the religious leaders, determined on eliminating a menace; the soldiers, who join in their master's fun; and, finally, the pathetic sight of Pilate and Herod clinging to each other for support in the face of this silent one. All of these throw Jesus' integrity into high relief: they try to slake their thirst anywhere but in the one place where humans really can drink, while Jesus turns always and only to God.

Now look at the calling of Paul. In his career, up to the moment of the encounter with Jesus, he was trying hard to slake that thirst for God; but only when he met Jesus was he able to see what it really meant. The story of Paul's encounter with Jesus is so important in Acts that Luke feels the need to tell it no less than three times.

Luke's version of the calling of Paul (Acts 9:1-19)

But Saul, still[1] breathing murderous threats against the Lord's disciples, approached the High Priest and asked for letters from him to Damascus, for the synagogues, so that if he should find anyone who was of The Way,[2] both men and women, he might bring them under arrest to Jerusalem.

1 This takes us back to his presence at, and consent to, Stephen's martyrdom (Acts 8:1).
2 One of Luke's words for the young Christian Church.

And as he was journeying, it happened that he was drawing near to Damascus and suddenly a light shone round him from heaven; and falling to the ground he heard a voice saying to him, 'Saoul, Saoul,[1] why are you persecuting me?'

And he said, 'Who are you, Lord?'[2]

He said, 'I am Jesus, whom you are persecuting.[3] But rise up and go into the city, and it will be told you what you must do.'

Now the men who journeyed with him stood speechless, because they heard the voice,[4] but saw nobody. Paul got up from the ground, but when he opened his eyes he could not see a thing. And they took him by the hand and led him into Damascus. And he was blind for three days, and he neither ate nor drank.[5]

And there was a certain disciple in Damascus named Ananias, and the Lord said to him in a dream, 'Ananias'.

And he said, 'Here I am, Lord.'

And the Lord said to him, 'Arise and go to the alley called "Straight", and seek in the house of Judas for a man of Tarsus called Saoul. For, see, he is praying, and he saw a man [in a vision] called Ananias, coming in and laying hands on him, so that he should see again.'

And Ananias replied, 'Lord, I have heard from many people about this man, what evil things he did to your saints in Jerusalem. And here he has authority from the high priests to arrest all those who call on your name.'[6]

✸ 1   For reasons that are not entirely clear, Luke uses in this story the Aramaic form of Saul's name when he is addressed by Jesus and by Ananias. It is a pleasing thought that this might be Paul's own reminiscence, transmitted to Luke, but there is no way of demonstrating that this is so.

2   'Kyrie': so Paul is in the right semantic region. The call has come from what he recognises as a superior power.

3   Notice the implication: Jesus is deeply identified with his Church.

4   Presumably the voice of Jesus, rather than of Paul; so the calling is a *public* event.

5   So a calling does not always leave you invigorated, ready for action.

6   We notice that the mere fact of having a calling does not mean that everyone will say, 'Welcome aboard'.

The Lord said to him, 'Go,[1] because this one is a chosen instrument, to carry my name before the Gentiles and kings and children of Israel. For I shall show him that he must suffer many things on behalf of my name.'[2]

Ananias went off, and entered the house, and laid his hands on him and said, 'Brother Saoul, the Lord has sent me, Jesus who appeared to you on the way by which you were going,[3] so that you might recover your sight, and be filled with the Holy Spirit.'[4]

And immediately there fell from his eyes [things] like scales, and he saw again, and he arose, and was baptised, and accepting some food he regained his strength.[5]

This story of how Paul found his thirst quenched probably owes something to Luke's gift as a storyteller. Now look at Paul's version of the same. He speaks with maddening brevity; but see how he radiates a certainty that his thirst really has been quenched.

Paul's own version of his call (1 Corinthians 15:1-11)

I remind[6] you, brothers and sisters, of the gospel which I gospelled to you, which you received, on which you take your stand, through which you are being saved, in what [manner of] speech[7] I gospelled you, if you hold it fast, unless perchance you believed in vain. For I passed on to you, as Item Number One, what I had also received, that Jesus Messiah died for our sins according to the Scriptures, and that he was buried, and that he

---

1 Part of the presupposition of the story is that both Paul and Ananias have easy dialogue with Jesus.
2 No one said it would be easy.
3 Travelling to Damascus, or persecuting the Church?
4 A key idea in Luke – Acts.
5 Perhaps compare Luke 8:55.
6 Literally, 'I make known to you'.
7 Literally, 'in what word'.

was raised on the third day according to the Scriptures, and that he appeared to Kephas,[1] then to the Twelve.[2] Then he appeared to upwards of 500 brothers and sisters at once, of whom the majority remain to this day, but some have fallen asleep. Then he appeared to Jacob, then to all the apostles. Last of all he appeared, as to one born untimely, even to me. For I am the least of the apostles, who am not fit to be called an apostle, because I persecuted the Church of God. But by the grace of God I am what I am, and his grace towards me has not been unprofitable, but I have laboured more abundantly than all of them, not I, but the grace of God with me. So, whether I or they, so we preach, and so you believed.

For Paul, what mattered above all was that in his encounter with Jesus he discovered what he had been looking for. From that moment, he was certain that Jesus had been raised by God from the dead, and Jesus became the Lord for whom he thirsted with every fibre of his being. It sometimes feels as though Paul can hardly compose a sentence without mentioning the name of his beloved. The above passage develops Paul's certainty (in the light of the Corinthians' uncertainty) about the Resurrection, which was the consequence of his certainty that he had indeed seen Jesus. Feel Paul's thirst in all that he says.

What most matters here for Paul is his absolute conviction that he has encountered Jesus, and that the Resurrection had really taken place. Nor is it just his encounter; but also, he reminds his Corinthians, people who knew Jesus well, who were 'thirsting' to see him again, were certain that they had seen Jesus after his death. That is the shape of our thirst.

---

1 Aramaic for 'Rock', i.e. Peter.
2 Not 'Eleven', as elsewhere; they have become an institution.

Three questions

- What are the false ways in which you have tried to slake your thirst?
- Have you known 'John's story' in your own life? In the lives of others?
- Do these texts speak to your experience? Which ones and why?

Closing Prayer

God our Father and Mother,
teach us to quench our thirst only in you,
so that we may share in the loving silence
of Jesus your Son.
Amen.

CHAPTER 2

Thirsting for Home

Opening Prayer

God and Lord of all,
make us aware how much we long for you,
how much we need the healing that you alone can give.
Teach us to accept nothing less than you,
in whom alone we find our home. Amen.

Home Lies ahead of Us

Because of this thirst that lies deeper in us than anything that we can imagine, we ache for restoration. The longing that is deep within us sometimes presents itself as nostalgia for an idyllic (and often illusory) past when everything was perfect, or for 'home'. Each of us feels the pain, but to ease it we must go forwards towards God, our true home, not backwards to 'where it was safe'. Our thirst is our desire to be 'restored', made whole again, and only God can do that; retiring into our shells cannot do it. As in Dylan's case, we have to move forwards, not backwards, if we are to find our way home.

Dylan's story

Dylan was the wicket-keeper of a cricket team which I helped to coach. An exuberant 15-year-old, he had the gift of remaining cheerful even under pressure; even when the opposition were three hundred for not very many, it was he who kept the team's spirits up. I was watching the rugby match at which he was injured, and saw that he was lying horribly still after a scrum collapsed. I had chatted to him that morning, and he was enormously proud that he was now the 1st XV's hooker. But Dylan's spine had been damaged, a nerve had been bruised, and he has not walked since. I can only say that I have never once heard him complain at his lot, and have marvelled at his refusal to look back in nostalgia, and his determination to look ahead and to 'get on with life'. He was not 'restored' in any physical sense, but his ability to see things in a completely new way was a most astonishing 'restoration', for himself and for those around him. He is utterly 'at home' in himself.

Our first story from the Gospels concerns a man who was very far from 'home'.

A demoniac finds his way 'home' (Mark 5:1-20)

And they came to the other side of the sea, to the land of the Gerasenes. And when he got out of the boat, immediately there met[1] him, coming out of the tombs, a man with an unclean spirit. He had made his home among the tombs.[2] Not even with handcuffs could anyone restrain him, because he had often been restrained with handcuffs and shackles, and the handcuffs and shackles had been torn apart and shattered by him.[3] And no one could tame him. And all night and all day he was in the tombs and in the mountains, crying out and bruising himself with stones.[4] And seeing Jesus from a long way off[5] he ran up and worshipped him;[6] and shouting out in a loud voice he says,

---

1 Mark focuses our attention on this striking encounter by his emphatic positioning of the verb.

2 This certainly means trouble. Jesus stands for life, and this man for death. And, moreover, where he lives, 'the tombs', is no place to be 'at home'.

3 We are meant to be frightened by this apparently irresistible power.

4 You could hardly imagine a person less 'at home'.

5 The reader will reflect that later on in this Gospel we shall find Peter (14:54) and the faithful women (15:40) at this range from Jesus. You might think about the differences.

6 Rather a remarkable thing?

'What is there between you and me, Jesus, Son of God Most High?[1] I adjure you by God, don't torment me.'

For Jesus kept saying to him, 'Come out, unclean spirit, out of the man.'

And he kept asking him, 'What is your name?'[2]

And he said to him, 'Legion[3] is my name; because we are numerous.' And he kept begging him, over and over again, not to send them out of the area. Now there was, there by the mountain, a great herd of pigs feeding, and they asked him, 'Send us into the pigs, so that we can enter them.' And he gave them permission. And the unclean spirits left [the man] and entered the pigs. And the herd rushed down the cliff into the sea, about two thousand of them, and they were drowned in the sea.[4] And their herdsmen ran away, and reported to the city, and to the farms: and they came to see what had happened.

And they came to Jesus, and they saw the one who had been possessed by demons, wearing clothes and in his right mind – the one who had had the Legion. And they were afraid.[5] And those who had seen [it] explained to them how it had happened with the possessed man, and about the pigs. And they began to beg him to go away from their borders.[6] And as he was going on board ship, the one who had been demonised was begging him that he might be with him.[7] And [Jesus] did not let him, but said

1 We notice that he is astonishingly 'at home' with Jesus, and identifies him quite correctly.

2 This is a decisive move in the battle.

3 The legion is the largest Roman infantry unit. When complete, it numbered 6000 men. So Mark is both stressing how appallingly possessed (hence not at home) the man was, and emphasising that the Roman occupation was more like a demonic possession than a gift of peace. We also notice, incidentally, that the great horde of unclean spirits have lost the battle; he has admitted his name.

4 We shall be missing the point of the story if we find ourselves pitying the great horde of pigs or their unfortunate owners. For Mark and his readers, pigs were unclean animals who made an ideal home for unclean spirits; and their rush into the sea would have been regarded as a thoroughly appropriate ending. They have 'gone home'!

5 So the formerly possessed man is 'at home'; but are the local inhabitants?

6 Suddenly 'home' looks uncomfortably different to them.

7 His reaction contrasts profoundly with that of the locals; he knows where 'at home' is. He also has the instincts of a disciple (see 3:14).

to him, 'Go to your home, and tell them what great things the Lord has done for you and how much mercy he has shown you.' And he went off and began to proclaim in the Decapolis how much Jesus[1] had done for him.

And they all marvelled.

This is a story that explains the meaning of what it is to be at home. Now comes another, and even better-known exploration of that powerful idea. It starts with a complaint about the kind of people with whom Jesus was at home, and who were at home with him.

A son who left home and returned; and another son who was always 'at home' – or was he? (Luke 15:1-3; 11-32)

And they were drawing near to listen to him, all the taxcollectors and sinners. And the Pharisees and scribes complained, 'This fellow offers hospitality to sinners, and has table-fellowship with them!' He told them this parable . . .

'A certain man had two sons. And the younger of them said to the father, "Father – give me the bit of the inheritance that falls to my share."[2]

'And he divided his life[3] between them.[4]

'Not many days later, the younger son gathered everything together, and went abroad to a remote country. And there he scattered the inheritance, living extravagantly. When he had spent the lot, there came a powerful famine all through that region, and he began to be in need. And he went and joined one of the citizens

---

1 Jesus is identified here as 'the Lord'. The man is really at home in the story.

2 This is every aggressive adolescent we have ever known, of course – but it is astonishingly dismissive of the father: 'you're as good as dead – get on with it' is the tone of his request.

3 This could also be translated as 'living' or even 'property'; but I have opted for a more literal version, to underline the father's generosity.

4 This should make us pause and stare.

of that place; and he sent him into his fields to feed the pigs.[1] And he was longing to fill his belly from the pods that the pigs were eating; but no one would give him anything.

'When he came to himself[2] he said, "How many of my father's employees are overflowing with food – and here am I dying of hunger![3] I shall arise and go to my father. And I'll tell him, 'Father – I have sinned against God and against you. I am no longer worthy to be called your son. Take me as one of your employees.'"

'And he got up and went to his father. And when he was still a long distance away, his father saw him[4] and had compassion on him,[5] and he ran and fell on his neck and kissed him.

'And the son told him, "Father – I have sinned against God and against you. I am no longer worthy to be called your son."[6]

'The father said to his slaves, "Quick! Bring out the best robe and put it on him. Put a ring on his finger, and sandals on his feet. Bring the calf we have been fattening, and sacrifice it. Let's eat and celebrate because this son of mine was dead and he's alive again; he was lost and he is found." And they began to celebrate.[7]

'Meanwhile, the elder son was in the field.[8] When he came [back] and got close to the house, he heard symphonies and dancing. And he summoned one of the servants and asked what all this was about.

'He told him, "Your brother has come, and your father has sacrificed the fattened calf, because he has got him back in good health."

---

1 We shudder at the thought – the son has not, after all, found himself at home.

2 The first part of the journey home.

3 The beginning of a new understanding of 'home'.

4 That is a shock we were not expecting: the unfailing gaze of God on the children he loves.

5 Another shock.

6 The son doesn't notice that 'home' has changed, and insists on making the speech that he has rehearsed. But his father knows better than to listen.

7 Home is quite astonishingly different.

8 The attentive reader sees the distant cloud that warns of a thunderstorm to come.

'He was enraged, and didn't want to go in; and his father went out to implore him.

'This was his answer to his father: "Look – all these years I'm slaving for you; I never transgressed a single commandment of yours, and you never even gave me a little goat[1] to celebrate with my friends.[2] But when this son of yours[3] comes, who has been eating up your life with prostitutes, you sacrifice the fattened calf to him."

'The father said to him, "Child, you are always with me; and everything that is mine is yours. It was essential to celebrate and rejoice, because this brother of yours[4] was dead, and is alive; he was lost and is found." '

Luke leaves us tantalised; does the older son go in and join the party? Decide for yourself, and see what that says about your understanding of 'home'.

The experience of alienation – part of a sandwich: (Mark 5:25-34)

And a woman who was with a flow of blood[5] for twelve years,[6] and suffered many things at the hands of many doctors, and had spent all that she had by her[7] and was in no way helped but

---

1 The elder brother has evidently forgotten that their father had already 'divided his life' between the two of them.
2 'Home' can be very deceptive; he was at the family house all the time, but was not at home, because the resentment was simmering inside him all the time.
3 In other words, 'no brother of mine'.
4 He is your brother – part of your 'home'!
5 This gynaecological disorder meant that she was alienated from ordinary human contact, and, we may guess, from herself. And from God?
6 As long as the child in the other part of the 'sandwich' had been alive; see Mark 5:42.
7 Mark gives a graphic picture of one who is quite at the end of her tether.

rather got to a worse state, hearing about Jesus, coming in the crowd from behind,[1] touched his garment.[2]

For she said, 'If I can touch his garments, I'll be saved.'[3]

And immediately[4] the fountain of her blood was dried up,[5] and she knew in her body[6] that she was healed[7] from her scourge.

And straightaway Jesus, recognising[8] in himself[9] that power had gone out of him, turning round in the crowd, said, 'Who touched my garments?'

And his disciples said to him, 'You see the crowd pressing on you, and you say, "Who touched me?"'

And he kept looking round to see the woman[10] who had done this.

And the woman,[11] in fear and trembling,[12] knowing what had happened to her, came, and fell before him and told him the whole truth.[13]

But he said to her, 'Daughter,[14] your faith has saved[15] you. Go in shalom, and be healthy[16] after your scourge.

---

1. For Mark, this phrase carries a hint of discipleship.
2. Thereby making Jesus ritually impure: the reader wonders what his reaction will be.
3. Notice that this is what she wants; the translations do not always manage to get it clear. Check to see how your translation renders this word.
4. A favourite adverb of Mark's.
5. Notice the characteristic crudeness of Mark's account.
6. Contrast this with the kind of knowledge that Jesus will shortly have.
7. Note that this is not the same as being 'saved', which we heard her wanting. Check to see how your translation renders this word.
8. This is the first time in the telling of the story that we have not been given the woman's point of view.
9. 'In himself': contrast this with the kind of knowledge that the woman has just had.
10. The translations do not often note that in the Greek it is clear that Jesus knew it was a woman.
11. Now we are back to her point of view, and will remain so until the end of the story.
12. The reader will think of those other brave women, at Mark 16:8.
13. The reader hangs in tense suspense: what will Jesus' reaction be to her honesty?
14. With this one word she is fully restored.
15. This, we remember, was what she was looking for at the beginning of the story. Check to see how your translation renders this word.
16. Check to see how your translation renders this word.

It may be worth mentioning that this striking story is 'sandwiched' by another story that is wrapped round it, the tale of Jairus' daughter (Mark 5: 22-24, 35-43). The evangelist surely intends us to read the two together, and to understand one by the other; I shall leave you to look at the other story for yourself. Just look, though, at this woman's plight. She is ritually impure, and has been so for twelve years. This means that technically she was not allowed to touch anybody, even in her family. So where could she possibly be at home with other people? And if she is not at home with other people, is she at home with herself? And if she is not at home with herself, how can she possibly be at home with God? Jesus' gift to her is therefore to 'bring her home'. Read the story as your story; let it tell you where you are 'not at home', and let it show you what is your 'way home'.

Three questions
- Do you think that you might have a longing for home?
- Do any of the texts speak to you of your longing?
- Have you seen these longings in others?

Closing Prayer

God, our Only True Light,
grant that we may always seek
to see only by your Light,
and to seek only for you. Amen.

CHAPTER 3

Thirsting for Direction

Opening Prayer

Lord, help us to hear your invitation,
help us to know that only your call
can give us the freedom for which we thirst. Amen.

How to Make Sense of Our Lives

One thing that human beings thirst for (though they may not always express it so) is a calling. I have a longing for a mast on which to nail my colours, a cause to make sense of my life. In the prison in which I work I notice that many of the prisoners wear tattoos indicating their allegiance to various causes: religious, patriotic, 'My Mum', or the name of a girlfriend (which can create a few problems when a new girlfriend appears). Consider the way people wear football shirts, although these are, it must be said, easier to change than tattoos: I was out of the United Kingdom while the 2002 Soccer World Cup was being played. When I left, everyone was wearing England football shirts; when I returned, and Brazil had won the Cup, it was the yellow of Brazil that predominated. The trick here is to make sure that the mast to which you nail your colours is, after all, the right one. The prisoners I serve are in prison because, in the majority of cases, they found that using drugs seemed to make sense of their lives. Others found this same kind of meaning in belonging to a gang. But you can't, as they have discovered, rely on these, and that they in fact lead nowhere. You can rely on God, of course, but somehow that can seem a great deal less obvious, and far less comforting.

My own call

I can still remember the moment when I knew that I had to join the Jesuits. I was, so it seemed to me then, and still seems, given no choice in the matter (perhaps I would never have got there on my own). One Christmas Eve when I was at university, just before Midnight Mass, I was kneeling in church, but not feeling particularly religious. I was wondering if I had time to nip out for a cigarette before the service started.

All I can say is that suddenly, without any mystical manifestations or angelic voices, I knew, beyond any shadow of doubt, and to my very great surprise, that the only thing I could do and be happy doing was to join the Jesuits. I was certainly not wondering what to do with my future (I was quite clear about that!) or seeking guidance: it just happened. This experience took place nearly 40 years ago, and the conviction has never left me; through all kinds of difficulties, my time of atheism, and the moments when I wondered if I should not after all get married, I could not gainsay that experience, which has remained for me an insistent, unchanging call, and the only way I can slake my thirst.

Now look at some of the calls recorded in the New Testament; make them your own stories. Where can your thirst be quenched? What will give you the direction for which you are longing? The next two stories are very striking indeed; have you known anything like them in your own life or in the lives of others?

The seekers (John 1:35-42)

On the next day, John [the Baptist] was standing again, with two of his disciples; and he looked intently at Jesus as he walked, and said, 'Look, the lamb of God!'[1] And his two disciples heard and followed Jesus.

Jesus turned and saw them following, and said to them, 'What are you looking for?'[2]

They said to him, 'Rabbi [which, when translated, means "Teacher"], where do you stay?'[3]

He says to them, 'Come and see.'[4] So they came; and they saw where he stayed. And they stayed with him that day (it was about the tenth hour).

Andrew, the brother of Simon Peter, was one of the two who had heard from John and had followed [Jesus]. He first found his own brother Simon, and said to him, 'We have found the Messiah.'[5] He led him to Jesus.

Jesus looked intently at him, and said, 'You are Simon, the son of John. You shall be called Cephas (which means "Rock").'[6]

Now for a similar story. Watch these two sets of brothers finding a very unexpected new direction in their life.

---

1 A mysterious phrase, which has nevertheless caught the Christian imagination and still appears regularly in Christian worship. Clearly it also snared the imagination of John's two disciples.

2 Remarkably, these are the first words attributed to the Word in the Gospel of John. It is an excellent question for each of us to allow the Lord to put to us.

3 The idea of 'staying', which includes both 'permanence' and 'indwelling', is very important in the Gospel of John. Notice that it is used three times in this passage. Could this help readers in their search for direction?

4 These words are addressed to all who read the Gospel, who seek direction.

5 Direction can come to us from God through other people.

6 The nicknaming implies a) that Jesus has private knowledge, and b) that his knowledge of Simon is intimate enough to suggest a jocular nickname (Simon was not all that 'rocklike').

Two sets of brothers (Mark 1:16-20)

> And going by the Sea[1] of Galilee, he saw Simon and Andrew[2] the brother of Simon, casting into the sea. For they were fishermen.[3]
>
> And Jesus said to them,[4] 'Come here, behind me,[5] and I shall make you fish for humans.'[6]
>
> And immediately, abandoning their nets, they followed[7] him.
>
> And going on a little bit further, he saw James of Zebedee and John his brother,[8] and [they were] in the boat putting their nets to rights.[9] And immediately[10] he called them.
>
> And abandoning[11] their father Zebedee in the boat with the hired men, they went behind[12] him.

This story is so familiar to us that we are no longer startled by it. Read it again, as though for the first time, and relish the shock it produces. In particular, look at the direction that their lives took thereafter, these two pairs of brothers. Tradition has it that the new direction led, through many failures and contradictions, to martyrdom. Do you think that they ever came to regret following this new direction?

Now look at what happened to Jesus as he started his ministry.

---

1 Something always happens 'by the sea' in Mark's Gospel.

2 The first mention in the Gospel of this pair. It is striking to me (though relatively few of the commentators seem to be struck by it) that Simon has a perfectly respectable Hebrew or Aramaic name, whereas 'Andrew' is Greek.

3 Notice the calmness of the scene; two men pursuing their familiar trade, and how sharply it contrasts with what follows.

4 It is often alleged that 'Jesus must have known them before'. Perhaps, but Mark does not say so, and that is what gives the story its sharp edge.

5 'Behind' is a word for discipleship in Mark.

6 A little joke, more characteristic of Jesus than we often suppose.

7 Another discipleship word in Mark.

8 These two and Simon, not Andrew of the Greek name, are to form Jesus' 'inner cabinet'.

9 Another scene of calm ordinariness; God *can* irrupt into our lives.

10 A favourite word of Mark, particularly in these opening chapters.

11 That word again.

12 That familiar discipleship word.

Jesus' search for direction in the desert (Mark 1:12-13 and parallels)

And immediately[1] the Spirit hurls him into the desert.[2] And he was in the desert for forty days,[3] being tested by the Satan,[4] and he was with the beasts[5] and the angels ministered to him.[6]

Matthew 4:1-11	Luke 4:1-13
Then Jesus was led up into the desert by the Spirit to be tested by the devil. And fasting forty days and forty nights, afterwards he was hungry (verses 1, 2).	And Jesus, full of the Holy Spirit, returned from the Jordan and was led by the Spirit in the desert for forty days being tested by the devil. And he did not eat anything in those days, and on their completion he was hungry (verses 1, 2).
And the Tempter approached and said to him, 'If you are the Son of God, say that these stones become loaves of bread.' But he replied and said, 'It is written: "Not by bread alone shall a human being live, but by every word coming out of God's mouth"' (3, 4).	And the devil said to him, 'If you are the Son of God, tell this stone to become bread.' And Jesus replied to him, 'It is written that not by bread alone shall a human being live' (3, 4).

1 This is a favourite adverb of Mark's in the first two chapters, giving an impressive sense of urgency.

2 This is stronger language than the versions often give. Sometimes it has to be like that.

3 The reader is meant, of course, to think of Moses (Exodus 34:28; Numbers 14:34) and of Elijah (1 Kings 19:8).

4 The 'Adversary', the one who aims to persuade humans to slake their thirst in the wrong place, in the wrong way.

5 No one really knows what this means, but look perhaps at Isaiah 11:6-9. Or, for a contrast, at Isaiah 13:21, 22; Psalm 22:12-21; Ezekiel 34:5, 8. Some of Mark's readers might have been reminded of Daniel in the lion's den (Daniel 6); a later generation will have thought of Christians being fed to the lions. And see perhaps 1 Peter 5:8-9.

6 This presumably means that we are to see Jesus as victorious over the temptation.

Then the devil takes him to the Holy City and sets him on the pinnacle of the Temple and says to him, 'If you are Son of God, then throw yourself down. For it is written that "he commands his angels about you and on [their] hands they will lift you up, lest you should strike your foot against a stone".' Jesus said to him, 'Again it is written, "You shall not tempt the Lord your God"' (5-7).

Again the devil takes him to an exceedingly high mountain and shows him all the kingdoms of the world and their glory. And he says to him, 'All these things I shall give to you, if you'll fall down and worship me.' Then Jesus says to him, 'Go, Satan. For it is written, "The Lord your God you shall worship, and him alone will you adore"' (8-10).

[Then the devil leaves him, and look! angels came and ministered to him (verse 11).]

And he led him to Jerusalem and set him on the pinnacle of the Temple and said to him, 'If you are Son of God, throw yourself down from here. For it is written that "he commands his angels about you to guard you and on [their] hands they will lift you up, lest you should strike your foot against a stone".' And Jesus replied and said to him, 'It is said, "You shall not tempt the Lord your God"' (9-12).

And leading him up he showed him all the kingdoms of the inhabited world in a moment of time, and the devil said to him, 'To you I shall give all this dominion and their glory. Because it is handed over to me. And to whom I want, I give the dominion to them. So, if you'll worship before me, it'll all be yours.' And Jesus answering said to him, 'It is written, "The Lord your God you shall worship, and him alone shall you serve"' (5-8).

[And having completed every temptation the devil departed from him until an opportune moment (verse 13).]

We need not make much here of the differences between the three accounts. We notice, though, the calm certainty of Mark that the Spirit can insist that Jesus undergo a time of testing by the Adversary, and that he be 'with the wild beasts'; but God does not abandon either Jesus or those who follow his way. Our thirst can be quenched in the desert; however, we cannot avoid experiencing the thirst.

In Matthew and Luke, the gospel tradition makes more explicit some of the (false) ways in which we can try and 'fill the gap'. The first is to (mis)use our gifts: Matthew and Luke do not doubt that Jesus could have made bread out of stones. And they are certain that he would have been wrong to do so, abusing his gifts for his own self-interest, even in the service of so basic a human right as eating. Jesus' reply, in the form of a quotation from Deuteronomy, points the reader in the direction of a God who alone can 'fill the gap' in our lives.

The second temptation (here I am following Matthew's order rather than Luke's) is a heady one: 'cast yourself down'. It conjures up all sorts of images in us including the deep desire, which is buried in most of us, to be able to fly. We are not, however, made this way, and it is no good hunting the Scriptures to pretend that we are. What is the 'gap-filler' on offer here? I suppose it is the temptation to perform the spectacular, eye-catching gesture, in the service of the Kingdom; but that is not how the Kingdom is built. The Kingdom is built in God's way, and 'you shall not tempt the Lord your God'.

The third temptation besets us all the time. We are forever being invited to put idols where God should be, at the centre of our lives. An idol is anything (other than God) that holds centre stage for us. We each can make our own list of the ways in which we keep God at bay, the foolish distractions with which we seek to quench our thirst for God. And not one of them works, not even when (as in this temptation) they can be given a plausible pretext of piety. For whether Jesus is being tempted by power (and that makes human beings behave in the oddest ways) or by the desire to achieve his

Father's project painlessly, it is still an idol, and will not give him what he is looking for.

Our next passage tells how Jesus gave much-needed direction to those puzzled disciples of his. Can the lesson here apply also to us?

The Spirit's mysterious guidance (Acts 16:6-10)

God is always there, giving us direction, even when it may not feel like it. In this remarkable episode, the early Church's preaching is given divine impetus to leap the geographically narrow, but culturally and psychologically huge, gap between Asia and Europe.

> They crossed through Phrygia, and the Galatian region, having been prevented by the Holy Spirit from preaching the word in Asia. Coming down to Mysia, they tried to travel into Bithynia, and the Spirit of Jesus didn't let them. Leaving Mysia on one side, they went down to Troas. And a vision in the night appeared to Paul: a Macedonian man was standing and begging him, 'Cross over into Macedonia and help us.' When he saw the vision, immediately we sought to go out into Macedonia, convinced that God had summoned us to evangelise them.

Chapter 16 of Acts speaks of the foundation of the Church at Philippi, perhaps Paul's favourite group of Christians. These verses tell us how the gospel came to be preached there. First, 'the Holy Spirit prevented' them from preaching in Asia. Second, 'the Spirit of Jesus didn't let them' go to Bithynia. Third, and more positively, there is a vision, giving definite direction: 'Cross over into Macedonia and help us.' Generally God's direction is not quite as obtrusive as these phrases imply (though Luke is a bit vague on the details). Or is it? Perhaps we need to be a good deal more attentive to the way God might be speaking directly to us, or through the people we meet, and those 'coincidences' that are not coincidences at all.

The attentive reader will note that this passage starts in the third person plural ('they') and ends in the first person plural ('we'). Perhaps the most obvious explanation is that Luke was with Paul for the four 'we' passages that are strung through the remaining chapters of Acts. Certainly they have a vividness that may suggest a first-hand account. Of course, the whole of Acts bears vivid testimony to the Spirit's direction of the gospel.

Answering the call is the only way in which we can slake our thirst; but it will be neither easy nor comfortable. Are you prepared for it?

Three questions
- Were you called? If so, was it all at once, or a slow, lingering process?
- Do you have any regrets about the call?
- Did the call quench your thirst?

Closing Prayer

God and Lord,
you call us and we have refused to hear.
Teach us that only in answering your invitation
can we quench our thirst.
Through Christ Our Lord. Amen.

CHAPTER 4

Thirsting for Holiness

Opening Prayer

God, Saviour and Redeemer
Holy of Holies,
teach us to long for your holiness
and never to falter in our quest for it. Amen.

Thirsting for What Is Real

What are believers for? If you read the newspapers, the general assumption is that they are either naïve or a menace. At best, it seems, they are do-gooders, whose only value is to make the world a better place, for example by feeding the hungry or looking after those who suffer from AIDS. Obviously, we must do these things, and believers have always done them. I should like to suggest, however, that our prime function is that of a signpost, pointing with trembling finger and uncertain eye to the presence of the Holy in our world. We (and not just the secular media) feel embarrassed at the idea of 'holiness'; and yet it is essential. For the holy is that in us which is the most real and the most reliable. It is the faintest hint of the mystery that is at the heart of life, that which makes us want to go down on our knees. This is the mystery that can be glimpsed in the lives of holy people.

It is hard to be precise about what holiness is. Certainly it is not the vinegar-faced rigour that some religious people feel compelled to adopt. Neither is it identical with regular churchgoing, as it may be found in those who do not go to church. What, positively, is it? One of the ingredients of holiness is a mature and warm humanity. Often this can (in my view *should*) go with a sense of humour that might be mistaken for flippancy (holy people are not very 'serious'). Maturity, though, is important. It has nothing to do with those forms of entertainment which are classed as 'adult' in our society (laughably so, since they are more aptly called 'early adolescent'). This maturity is hard-won, and *never* comes without suffering; the difference is that in holy people the suffering has brought neither bitterness nor dumb resignation, but a full-grown humanity. Most of all, and quite unconsciously, it points to the Transcendent, the deepest reality, which we only partly glimpse out of the corner of our eye, but which is, nevertheless, profoundly real, which we call God. With all our being we thirst for holiness.

Holy places and persons

It is hard to find a single anecdote that captures the flavour. Negatively, we might start with the judgement passed, in living memory, by one famous English Jesuit on another, 'Very holy,' he said, 'quite pathetic!' I can think of places where I sensed the holy: the Grotto at Lourdes, especially late at night, always seemed to me, even in my moments of profoundest unbelief, to have that numinous quality. The same is true of two places that I disliked on first acquaintance, St Peter's in Rome, and the Church of the Holy Sepulchre in Jerusalem. The two of them, after my first repulsion, turned out to have that quality, despite the all-too-evident traces of human sinfulness that surround them and besmirch their history: for it is precisely in our human mess that great holiness is found. Perhaps it was simply the fact that people had been praying there for centuries.

Or I think of an old Zulu lady who has endured all that life can throw at her: a husband's death, a son's exceptionally wayward behaviour, persecution by a local warlord (who thought himself safe from the consequences), a brother-in-law whose offer of marriage had to be violently rejected, another son who died of AIDS. You can see in her face, and in the remarkable quality of her smile, the accumulated wisdom that all this, prayerfully endured, has produced. She has seen it all, and has won through. She is a person of great warmth and humour, and great wisdom (I swiftly learnt to respect her assessment of people). She also has the precious quality of openness to the transcendent, though she would raise a quizzical eyebrow were I to attempt to translate that very Western idea into Zulu; and it was not just that she is a practising Christian; rather it is that she is a woman of prayer, 'on terms with God'. She would unobtrusively drop into our chapel in her lunch-hour, 'for a spot of socialising', as one of the brethren put it; and also, when the spirit led her that way, she was not ashamed to qualify as a sangoma (or 'traditional healer'). The most striking thing about her is her humanity. Holiness does not mean ceasing to be human.

Then there was my father. This is quite private, and I broach it with considerable reservation; nor shall I tell you everything. I remember, however, how he was just three weeks before he died. We were all on pilgrimage together in Lourdes, working for the sick, and I recall all the unwise things he cheerfully did (he had suffered a serious coronary some ten years earlier), pushing the sick pilgrims around on heavy trolleys, or pulling their cumbersome bath chairs, including the long climb up the hill to their hospital, praying the Rosary all the while, but greeting people with a wink as he passed. And he was happy in this, and touched by God's gift of humour. Less than two weeks after we returned from that pilgrimage he was dead, a major heart attack brought on by running for a train. Did his work in Lourdes contribute to that? Undoubtedly. Would he have cared? Not for a moment. Holiness does not count the cost. But does it make sense?

See now how Paul views reality. The only thing that matters, he has discovered, is 'to be found in Christ'; and he uses very strong language in saying so.

Thirsting for holiness and maturity (Philippians 3:7-14)

But whatever profit I had, those were the things that I regarded as loss on Christ's account.

As a matter of fact, I regard everything as loss on account of the supreme good of knowing Christ Jesus my Lord, on whose account I lost everything.

And I regard it all as dung in order to have Christ on my profit account, and in order to be found in Christ.

I want to have no righteousness based on Law; the righteousness I want is that based on Christ's faith, the righteousness that comes from God, to faith: to know him and the power of his Resurrection, as well as the solidarity of his sufferings, being shaped to his death, so that perhaps, somehow, I may get to reach the Resurrection from the dead.

It's not that I've already got it, or that I'm already made perfect. But I'm chasing it, and perhaps I might snatch the prize, just at the moment when I am snatched by Christ as his prize.

Fellow-Christians: I don't suppose that I've snatched it. I simply forget about the laps that I have already run, and I'm bracing myself for the laps that are still to come. I'm going for the finish, for the gold medal. That is what I call my 'upward calling' from God in Jesus Christ.

Paul speaks passionately here, in this piece of intimate autobiography. Sometimes we dismiss holiness as something pale and weedy. Paul's version of it is robust, loving, and compellingly human. He was never anything else, this difficult and prickly person who seems to have quarrelled with practically everyone he worked with. Holiness does not mean that we lose our human angularities, only that we continue to find our way, through them and despite them, to the God for whom we thirst, the One who alone is the Real Thing.

Holiness does not at first sight make sense; but when you look a little deeper it does, once you learn to see things upside-down. Consider the shock and the wisdom of the Beatitudes. This list of people who are counted as happy is a thoroughly subversive one, and if we skip too rapidly over those on it, we shall miss their radical nature. Matthew seems to have placed them at the beginning of his account of Jesus' Sermon on the Mount quite deliberately, in order to catch our attention; but they also function as his description of Jesus, the holy one who points unfailingly in the direction of what is real and holy. If we read the Beatitudes carefully, they should make us thoroughly uncomfortable: are they *really* lucky, those who are poor, mourning, meek, persecuted and the like? Stay with this text, and try to see the deep sanity that underlies it.

Turning the world upside-down (Matthew 5:1-12)

Seeing the crowds, he went up on to the mountain, and when he sat down his disciples approached him. And opening his mouth he began to teach them, saying:[1]

'Congratulations[2] to the poor in spirit[3] – for theirs is the Kingdom of Heaven.

Congratulations to those who are grieving – for they shall be comforted.

Congratulations to the gentle – for they shall inherit the earth.

Congratulations to those who hunger and thirst for justice[4] – for they shall be sated.

Congratulations to the merciful – for they shall be mercied.[5]

---

1 Note the very formal beginning, and the effect it has on the reader. Note too, how the evangelist starts with three expressions for 'utterance': 'opening his mouth', 'began to teach', and 'saying'.

2 Not everyone would translate it this way; generally translators prefer 'happy' or 'blessed'; but at least it may make us stop and think. Someone recently suggested to me the translation 'how lucky . . .' to bring out the shock value. Or what about 'how fortunate'?

3 Some translate this 'those who know their need of God'.

4 God's justice: the world as it was intended to be.

5 This translation attempts to convey something of the sound of the original. The word for mercy is connected with the familiar 'eleison', and with the root of 'olive oil', used to soothe the wounds of warriors and athletes' bruises. See also what the Good Samaritan did, in Luke 10:34. This Beatitude is dramatised in Matthew 18:23-35.

Congratulations to the pure in heart – for they shall see God.

Congratulations to the peacemakers – for they shall be called sons[1] of God.

Congratulations to those who are persecuted for the cause of justice – for theirs is the Kingdom of Heaven.[2]

Congratulations to you when they revile you and hassle you and bad-mouth you for my sake.

Rejoice and be glad – for your reward is great in Heaven.

For that's how they reviled the prophets who went before you.'

The only proper response to this extraordinary text is a stunned silence, as we digest Jesus' cheerful and eccentric command to 'rejoice and be glad' as he congratulates us on being 'reviled and hassled'. Some people suggest that the way to appreciate this list of congratulations is to compile your own list of 'the world's congratulations': 'Congratulations,' it might run, 'to the rich and well-educated, to those who are having a good time, to those who trample all over the opposition, who tell themselves "be realistic", who have an eye for the main chance, who are universally acclaimed.' And so on. Who do you think is right here?

Then there is Jesus' own behaviour. We can get so distracted by the idea that Jesus is God that we lose sight of his humanity; and human beings, if we are to grow as we are supposed to grow, and to make of our lives what God wants us to make of them, need to pray, to feed our yearning for holiness by contact with the holy. See how Jesus operated after a busy day.

Jesus at prayer (Mark 1:35-38)

And early in the morning, while it was still very dark, he got up, went out, and went off to a wilderness place. And there he was

---

1 I have left the original, but we may think 'children' to ourselves. Matthew often sounds more exclusive of women than perhaps he means to be.

2 Just like the poor in spirit.

praying. And Simon and his friends hunted him down. And they
found him and they tell him, 'They're all looking for you.'
    And he says to them, 'Let's go elsewhere, to the nearby market
towns. For that was the reason I came out.'

Notice Jesus' response to Simon's insensitivity. He neither says,
'Don't interrupt, I'm praying!' as we might be tempted to do, nor
does he grudgingly agree to return with them. Instead, his mission
takes on a new direction. That kind of flexibility is what prayer
can do for you. Holiness enables us to overcome our instinctive
resistances and to live as we are called to live.

Now watch what holiness *does*. This next story does not belong
with John's Gospel; as you will see, if you let your eye run from the
end of chapter 7 to 8:12, it interrupts the flow. And if
you have one of those modern bibles with good study notes,
you will see other reasons for thinking that it does not belong
here. Nevertheless, the Jesus who is the hero of this story speaks
with the unmistakable accents of the New Testament's Lord, and
we must be grateful to whoever it was who was determined that
this story should not be lost to us. Holiness is not trapped in blind
observance of the rules, but sees real people in real (and not always
very simple) situations.

Holiness in action (John 8:1-11)

    . . . and Jesus went on to the Mount of Olives.
    And early on he again appeared in the Temple, and the whole
crowd came to him, and he sat down and began to teach them.
    And the scribes and the Pharisees bring a woman who had
been caught in adultery;[1] and setting her in the middle they

---

1 Someone is missing; since it takes 'two to tango', we cannot help asking why her male
partner is not present.

say to him, 'Teacher, this woman was caught in the act of committing adultery. Now in the Torah Moses commanded us to stone women such as this. So – what do you say?' (They said this by way of a test for him, in order to have grounds for an accusation against him.)

Jesus, however, bent down, and with his finger started writing on the ground.[1] But as they persisted in asking him, he straightened up[2] and said to them, 'Let the sinless one among you be the first to throw a stone at her.' And again he bent down and went on writing on the ground.

And when they heard it, they went out, one by one, starting with the elders.

And he was left quite alone,[3] just him, and the woman who had been put in to the middle. And Jesus straightened up[4] and said to her, 'Woman – where are they? Did no one condemn you?'

And she said, 'No one, Lord.'

And Jesus said, 'Neither do I condemn you. Go . . . and from this moment, don't sin any more.'

This lovely but subversive story catches the quality of Jesus' holiness, and perhaps also gives us a glimpse of the holiness he elicited in those he dealt with: the woman, obviously, stunned by what has not happened to her; but also, something happened to his opponents, who 'walked away'. Jesus' holiness enables him to see human beings, not adulterers (even when, as in this case, they are set out, like a staked goat, to catch a Bengal tiger); and it is what gives that special quality to his relationships. Holiness makes you more human, not less.

---

1 Scholarly (and other) imagination has been quite unrestrained in surmising what he might have been writing; but the text does not tell us.

2 This word is closely connected with the one previously used for 'bent down; but it is impossible to express this in translation into English.

3 Presumably the crowd he had been teaching also vanished.

4 Same root as before.

Three questions
- Have you known anyone you would regard as holy? What did you make of them?
- How do you feel in the presence of the holy?
- What would happen to our world if holiness were let loose in it?

Closing Prayer

Holy God,
we ask you to captivate us with your holiness.
May it radiate in our lives
and shine forth in our world. Amen.

CHAPTER 5

Thirsting To Serve

Opening Prayer

Lord, you have created us
to serve you and each other.
Teach us the wisdom of service
and the joy of opening out to other people,
just like your Son.
Amen.

The Way We Are Made

Something I have often noticed in Lourdes, and wherever the young, healthy and willing look after those who are 'physically challenged', is that the helpers receive – often to their surprise – far more than they give.

We human beings are created to serve. We say this, and nod wisely – but be careful. When preparing this talk, I had more or less resolved to start with this insight, not exactly one of breathtaking originality, when the telephone rang. It was another member of my community, asking for my immediate help in a tedious, unforeseen (by me, at any rate) and time-consuming task. My first reaction? It would be good to be able to report that I said, 'Coming, Lord', laid down my pen then and there, and went cheerfully off to serve the brethren. But I regret to say that, instead, I heard a voice inside me saying, 'My work is for God, and therefore far more important than this service to the community.' Happily, I realised what was going on, and was able to laugh at myself, though even then the best I could manage was a rather grudging: 'I'll be with you in ten minutes.'

We especially need to watch this tendency of ours to say, 'I'm more important than you.' Because if I *am* more important than you, then (especially if I am working for God) it doesn't matter what I do to you. I can declare war on you because you are 'bad' or 'the enemy'. If, on the other hand, everyone who crosses my path is someone whom the Lord invites me to serve, then my attitude may be different.

At this juncture it may be worth pointing out that here I am talking primarily about men; the male instinctively leans in the direction of domination, and that tendency needs correction. Women, on the other hand, often tend to lean in the direction of over-submissiveness, and for them the ideal of service may turn them into doormats. So these reflections are no more than an invitation to consider: if the cap fits, wear it.

'To serve them all my days'

The above is also the title of a novel[1] about a dedicated schoolmaster, which I came across when I was myself a schoolmaster. The novel (which was later televised) is an account of how the schoolmaster lived out this ideal of service, and in so doing found healing. It was, however, the title that struck me, and I realised that it gave me a clue as to how to make sense of what I was doing. For the inexperienced schoolmaster lives in terror of not being able to keep order (at least this one did), and is therefore inclined to impose 'savage sanctions' (my first pupils report that this was a phrase often on my lips, and a concept frequently put into practice!) in order to establish 'who's in charge around here'. Children need to know who is in charge, but I became aware that if my aim were to serve them, then the 'feel' of

---

1   By R. F. Delderfield.

my interaction with them would not be the same as if I were just trying to control them. And then, even if I were to employ 'savage sanctions', it would not have the same overtone as it would if I were fearfully trying to establish my place in the pecking-order. I do not say that I have always managed to live out this desire to serve, nor that my pupils would always have described how I taught them as service; but that was the goal that I wobbled towards.

The other part of the title was important, too: 'all my days'. My students were not just to be tiresome nuisances to whom I could bid a relieved farewell at the end of the class, term, year or school career; instead, I had taken them on for life, so that at any time in the future they could come to me for help, should the Lord so guide them (and perhaps I also could go to them for help. That seemed to make sense. What we have to embrace is a readiness to put others first and so (astonishingly enough) to discover ourselves for who we really are.

Not too grown-up (Mark 10:13-16)

> And they were bringing him children for him to touch them. But the disciples scolded them. But seeing [this], Jesus was angry, and said to them, 'Let the little children come to me. Do not prevent them, for of such is the Kingdom of God. Amen I tell you, whoever does not receive the Kingdom of God as a child, no way can they enter into [that Kingdom].' And taking them in his arms, he blessed [the children], laying his hands on them.

Jesus has this astonishing ability to open out to others, so he never thinks himself too important to deal with children; he is 'at their service'. Our danger is the opposite one, that instead of serving others we use them as stepping-stones. Later in the same chapter Jesus explains that:

'The Son of Man is going to be handed over to the Chief Priests and the scribes, and they will condemn him to death, and hand him over to the Gentiles. And they will make fun of him, and spit on him, and whip him, and they'll kill him.' (Mark 10:33-34)

Still, however, the disciples don't get it, and 'the sons of Zebedee' come asking, not for the privilege of serving, but for the best places in the Kingdom (10:35-40). This is followed by irritation on the part of the other ten (10:41), and the context makes it quite clear that they are cross, not because James and John have failed to grasp Jesus' teaching, but because they might have got their bids in early.

You can almost hear the weariness in Jesus' voice has he explains this service business to them again:

Not to be served but to serve (Mark 10:42-45)

And Jesus summoned them and said to them, 'You know that the so-called rulers of the Gentiles Lord[1] it over them, and their great ones tyrannise[2] over them. Among you it's not like that – instead, whoever wants to be Great among you will be your Servant. And whoever wants to be Number One among you will be everyone's Slave. You see, the Son of Man did not come to be served, but to serve, and to give his life as a ransom for many.'

Paul knows the truth of this. Writing to the Philippians, who were perhaps his favourite Church, but among whose members dissension was not unknown, he warns them:

---

1 I have capitalised this word because it contains the idea of Kyrios, the exalted title that the earliest Christians gave to Jesus, and which sycophantic admirers were starting to accord to the Roman emperors at this stage.

2 Difficult to get it right; the word here is connected with the idea of authority. In Mark, Jesus is really the only one with 'authority'.

Think of others as your superiors (Philippians 2:1-5)

So if there is any encouragement in Christ; if there is any consolation of love; if there is any communion of the Spirit; if there is any affection and compassion, fill up my joy, and [all] think along the same lines. Have the same love. Be unanimous, with just a single thought. Don't think anything for personal advantage or from empty conceit. Instead, in lowliness of mind, think of others as your superiors. Don't be each of you looking for your own interests – instead, look out for each other's interests. Among yourselves have the frame of mind that was in Christ Jesus.

And you can read for yourselves (Philippians 2:5-11) the beautiful hymn that follows, and which explains Christ Jesus' 'frame of mind', the attitude of unselfish service that must be ours.

Jesus' example (John 13:1-17)[1]

Before the feast of the Passover, Jesus, knowing[2] that the hour had come for him to transfer from this world to the Father,[3] having loved those who were his own in the world, loved them to the end.[4] And during supper, the devil, having already put it into the heart of Judas Iscariot that he should betray him,[5] [Jesus] knowing that the Father had given everything into his hands, and that he had come from God and was going to God,[6] arises from

---

1 Significantly, the evangelist puts this, and not the story of Jesus' institution of the Eucharist, at the head of his account of Jesus' last hours.
2 The Greek reads, more awkwardly, 'knowing, Jesus . . .' 'Knowing' is a very important idea in the fourth Gospel, and here the evangelist is giving it emphasis.
3 In other words, the gesture of service that follows is one of immense significance, a 'last will and testament'.
4 So we are are now about to see what love means in practice.
5 So service is not just to be offered to those who are gratifyingly responsive.
6 The fact that our destination and origin are with God does not exempt us from the command to serve.

supper and takes off his clothes, and taking a linen cloth, tied it round himself.[1] Then he throws water into the bowl and began to wash the feet of the disciples, and to wipe [them] with the linen cloth that he had tied round himself.

And so he comes to Simon Peter and Peter. He says to him, 'Lord – are you washing my feet?'[2]

Jesus answered and said to him, 'What I am doing you do not know now – but you will understand after it's all over.'[3]

Peter says to him, 'No way will you wash my feet – ever.'

Jesus answered him, 'If I don't wash you, you have no part with me.'

Simon Peter says to him, 'Lord, [then] not just my feet, but also my hands and my head.'[4]

Jesus says to him, 'The one who has been washed has no need to have anything but their feet washed – but they are completely clean. Even you are clean – but not all of you.' (For he knew his betrayer; because of that he said, 'You are not all clean.')[5]

So when he had washed their feet and taken his clothes and lain down again, he said to them, 'Do you know what I have done for you?[6] You people call me "Teacher" and "Lord", and this is well said,[7] for [that is what] I am. So – if I have washed your feet – [I who am your] "Lord" and "Teacher", you too ought to wash each other's feet. For I have given you an example, that as I have done for you, you also should do. Amen, Amen I

---

1 Jesus is rather making an exhibition of himself here, we should note with alarm.

2 The tone of this question suggests that Peter is not unduly impressed by his master's example.

3 If I had said this to my pupils, they probably would have been at least as incredulous as Peter.

4 The impetuous exaggeration reveals (what we always knew) that Simon's heart is in the right place.

5 Once again, it seems that we are expected knowingly to give service even to those who we know will fling it in our face.

6 We should be listening carefully now; Jesus is evidently about to give us an explanation of this extraordinary action.

7 Literally, 'You speak beautifully'.

tell you, a slave is not greater than his Lord, or an apostle[1] greater than the one who sent him. If you understand these things, congratulations if you do them.'

A spot of racial tension, resolved by service (Acts 6:1-7)

Immediately before the following incident of racism in Acts, Luke has given us the impression (see Acts 5:42) that everything was always perfect in the early Church, which, of course, makes us feel quite inadequate. This story of service reminds us that it was not always so simple.

> In those days, as the disciples multiplied, there arose a grumble[2] between the Greek-speakers and the Aramaic-speakers,[3] because the [Greek-speakers'] widows were being overlooked in the daily service.[4] So the Twelve summoned the group of the disciples and said, 'It is not desirable for us to abandon the word of God and serve at tables.[5] Instead, brothers [and sisters], select seven men among yourselves, who are attested, full of the Spirit and wisdom; and we shall appoint them for this need. Meanwhile we shall continue our engagement in prayer and the service[6] of the word.'
>
> And the word was pleasing [to] the entire group. And they chose Stephen, a man full of faith and the Holy Spirit, and Philip, and Prochorus and Nicanor and Timon and Parmenas and

---

❈ 1 Literally, 'One who is sent'.

2 The Greek word is the splendid-sounding *gongysmos*.

3 Literally, 'Hellenists' and 'Hebrews'. This is simple, old-fashioned racial tension in the Church.

4 In the days of no social welfare, widows and orphans were of course entirely dependent on the generosity of others. The Jews had an excellent system of support, but by now we may suspect that the Christians were no longer eligible for it; the differences between Jews and Christians would be starting to show.

5 This does not, of course, mean that the parish pastor is exempt from washing the dishes! The apostles' 'service' was different.

6 Notice that this is the third time the word 'service' or 'serve' has appeared in the passage.

Nicolaus (a proselyte of Antioch),[1] and they put them before the apostles. And they prayed and laid hands on them.

And the word of God grew and the number of disciples in Jerusalem increased very much. And a great crowd of priests were obedient to the faith.

Service of others, service of God (Romans 12:1-15)

In this next passage, Paul has completed the difficult section of the argument of Romans in support of his understanding of what God has done in Christ, including God's plan for Jews and Gentiles in Christ. But what does it mean in terms of practical living?

So I beg you, brothers and sisters, through the mercy of God, to offer your bodies as a living and holy sacrifice that is pleasing to God your rational service of worship.[2] And don't *con*form to this age: instead, be *trans*formed with a totally new outlook. This will enable you to test what God's will is, that which is good and pleasing and perfect.

For this is what I'm saying, through the free gift that has been given to me: don't go thinking high-and-mighty thoughts above and beyond what you ought to be thinking. Instead, your thoughts should be appropriate thoughts, mature thoughts, each one of you in accordance with the measure of faith that God has measured out.

You see, just as in a single body we find a number of limbs, and not all the limbs have the same function, that's how it is with us who are in Christ. There are lots of us, but we are each other's limbs.

We have been given different kinds of gifts according to the

---

1 These have impeccably Greek names; but in case you think that this is a merely political solution to the problem, note that the only two of these whom we ever hear of again are found, not 'serving at table', but preaching the gospel, to Judea, Samaria and Africa.

2 We notice here the liturgical language that Paul uses: the service of God and service of others cannot be separated.

grace that has been given us. If it is prophecy let it be proportionate to the faith; if it is service – then it should be exercised in service. It might be a teacher – then the gift would be exercised in teaching. It might be a comforter – then the gift should be exercised in comforting. It might be in contribution – then that should be done with single-minded generosity. If someone gives aid, let them be in earnest. An almsgiver should be cheerful about it. Love should not be a matter of acting a part. You should hate what is evil, and stick to what is good. You should love each other as brothers and sisters. You should take the lead in giving each other honour. Don't be reluctant in your commitment – be aflame with the Spirit. Be the Lord's slaves. Rejoice in hope. Stand fast when it's difficult. Take your share of the needs of the saints. Make a thing of hospitality. Bless your persecutors. [I say:] bless them, not curse them! Rejoice with those who rejoice, weep with those who weep.

This is an extraordinary passage. Service is a seamless garment – you can't say, 'Now I'm serving God; next I'll serve others.' The very specific detail to which Paul descends shows that what God has done in Christ changes us, so that we become people-for-others, opening out to God and (in the same breath) to other people.

In many countries, those who administer the system are called 'civil servants', and it is ruefully pointed out that they are sometimes neither civil nor servants. We should pray that people will not be able to say the same of us. We need to recognise our thirst to serve, and then allow ourselves to be taken over by it.

Three questions
- Can you remember a time when, perhaps unexpectedly, you found that serving 'quenched your thirst'?
- Can service be dehumanising?
- Can God be said to be 'at our service'?

Closing Prayer

Lord, teach us to be generous,
to serve you as you deserve;
to give and not to count the cost
to fight and not to heed the wounds
to toil and not to seek for rest,
to labour and to ask for no reward,
save that of knowing we do your holy will. Amen.

CHAPTER 6

Thirsting Across Boundaries

Opening Prayer

Lord, teach us that in you there is no distinction,
of race or gender or social status,
but that all are one in Christ. Amen.

The Unity of the Human Race

God did not create the artificial divisions that separate human beings. This is humanity's doing; for we create these 'boundaries' as a way of sheltering from our own insecurities, or thirst. In South Africa we have learnt to give this 'division-making' the justly reviled name of apartheid. I am told that, according to our DNA, all human beings, of whatever 'race', are more closely related than two groups of gorillas inhabiting adjacent valleys in central Africa. The Christian dispensation enables us to recognise any fellow-human as our brother or sister; I would argue that we thirst to see others as fellow-travellers rather than threats.

The South African elections

No one who was there will ever forget 27 April 1994 in South Africa, the day of our first democratic elections. The lead-up had not been promising. A key party in the negotiations had refused to come into the elections. Every day we listened to the BBC World and African News, and breathed a sigh of relief on the rare occasions when South Africa, and in particular our part of South Africa, was not mentioned. I was a District Observer for the elections, and had rather encouraged the students of the seminary, of which I was then Acting President, to act as Observers and Monitors, and now found myself wondering whether in doing so I had signed their death warrants, for there were threats of violence against anyone who worked for the elections in that area. Ten days before the elections, however, the missing party came into the process; one of the reasons for this, I am certain, was a great deal of prayer on all sides. And so we faced the day itself with enormous confidence. Nor was our confidence misplaced.

As a District Observer, I had seven polling stations to observe, and over the two days of the election, I drove about between them, watching the miracle happen at first hand. There were bent, old women on the road as early as 4am, determined, no matter how far they had to hobble, to register their votes; there were farmers taking their workers to the polls in their pick-up trucks; and there were the queues.

In the dark of the early morning it was exceedingly cold, for it was autumn, but as the day went on it became very hot. Everywhere I went, I could see black people and white people queuing together (a new experience for all of them) in the hot sun and talking to each other (a new experience for many of them). They queued for hours, and as they talked, the whites discovered a new continent for the first time.

Two things were clear: the blacks had a new freedom, so that they walked with pride that day, and the whites, given a new liberation, were able to shed the crippling burden of guilt. It would be silly to pretend that all our problems are behind us in South Africa, for they are not. Nevertheless, it was a miracle that we witnessed that day, and we can still feel its effects. The fact was that on that day God gave us a glimpse of our common humanity, which something very deep in us longs to recognise; it longs to reach out across man-made boundaries to our brothers and sisters on the other side of the fence.

The principal text that I shall use here is that of the Samaritan woman in John, Chapter 4, which meditates rather more widely on the idea of 'thirsting' and the connected idea of 'water'.

Jewish men do not have intercourse with Samaritan women (John 4:1-42)

Before we read the text, two words of explanation are in order. The first concerns the heading. This is not how verse 9 of Chapter 4 is ordinarily translated, but it is a possible translation, and it makes part of the point that this story seeks to put across. The second word of explanation concerns something called 'Johannine irony'. Again and again in the Fourth Gospel, it happens that Jesus is in dialogue with someone. That person fails to understand what Jesus is saying, but the reader knows perfectly well what is meant.

So there is a kind of conspiracy between the evangelist and the reader, from which Jesus' dialogue-partner is excluded, and which we call 'Johannine irony' – for example, Nicodemus (3:1-10) and Pilate (18:33-38). The 'irony' serves to make the point that Jesus really belongs elsewhere, and only 'his own' really understand him (1:11-13). Johannine irony points to a God who is just beyond our meanings, and to a Jesus who likewise challenges our understanding. Perhaps the key line in the story is 'my food is to do the will of the one who sent me'. That is the reality for which we hunger and thirst.

> So when Jesus knew that the Pharisees had heard that Jesus was making more disciples, and baptising more of them than John (and yet Jesus himself did not baptise; it was his disciples who did that), he left Judea and went off back to Galilee.
>
> He had to go through Samaria. So he came to a city of Samaria called Sychar, near the place that Jacob had given to Joseph his son. There was there the well of Jacob. So Jesus, worn

out[1] from the journey, sat, just like that, on the well. It was about the sixth hour.[2]

There comes a woman from Samaria to draw water. Jesus says to her, 'Give me a drink.' For his disciples had gone off to the city in order to buy food.[3] So the Samaritan woman says to him, 'How is that you, who are a Jew, are asking for a drink from me, who am a Samaritan and a woman?' (For Jewish men do not have intercourse with Samaritan women.)

Jesus replied and said to her, 'If you had known the gift of God, and who it is who is saying to you "give me a drink",[4] you would have asked him, and he would give you non-stagnant[5] water.'

She says to him, 'Lord,[6] you have no bucket either, and the spring is deep; so from where do you have this non-stagnant water? Can you possibly be greater than our father Jacob,[7] who gave us the well, and he drank from it himself and his sons and his domestic animals?'

Jesus replied and said to her, 'Whoever drinks of this water will be thirsty again. But whoever drinks of this water which I shall give them, will never be thirsty for eternity. Instead, the

---

1 The Greek word for this is from a root meaning 'hard work' and (by an obvious extension) 'weariness' that will appear several times in this episode.

2 Midday: as in Africa, so in the Ancient Near East, this is not the time to come to draw water. So, from the start, there is obviously something odd about the story. Why does the woman not come to draw water with all the other women?

3 The oddity continues. Firstly, in the Old Testament, a meeting of a man and a woman by a well again and again leads to betrothal. So there are sexual, or at least romantic, undertones running through the story. See Jack Miles, *Christ: A Crisis in the Life of God*, pp. 69-75 (William Heinemann, 2001). We need to grasp this in order to appreciate how, at the end, the woman's real thirst is in fact quenched. Secondly, the evangelist has neatly got the disciples (who will appear later as an important counterpoint to the woman) off-stage in order to allow for this man-woman encounter.

4 Here the woman is being introduced to First Steps in Christology, the main question of the Fourth Gospel: Who is this Jesus (and where is he from)?

5 Literally, 'living water', so it also carries a hint of the water of life.

6 Greek: Kyrie, which can mean 'Sir' or 'Lord'. It is a correct form of address for believing Christians to use towards Jesus, so she is doing well in her Christology lessons.

7 A very good question.

water which I shall give them will become in them a fountain of water bubbling up into eternal life.'[1]

The woman says to him, 'Lord, give me this water, so that I may not be thirsty, and not come here to draw water.'

He says to her, 'Go and call your man[2] and come here.'

The woman replied and said to him, 'I have no man.'

Jesus says to her, 'You have put it well, saying, "I have no man", for you have had five men, and the one you have now is not your man. This you have spoken truly.'

The woman says to him, 'Lord, I see that you are a prophet.[3] Our ancestors worshipped on this mountain; and you people say that in Jerusalem is the place where one must worship.'

Jesus says to her, 'Believe me, woman, that the hour is coming when neither on this mountain nor in Jerusalem will you people worship the Father. You people worship what you do not know, whereas we worship what we do know, because salvation is from the Jews. Instead, the hour is coming, and now is, when true worshippers will worship the Father in spirit and in truth.[4] For the Father is seeking[5] for people of this sort, who worship him. God is spirit, and those who worship God must do so in spirit and in truth.'

The woman says to him, 'I know that the Messiah is coming, the one called "Christ". When he comes, he will announce everything to us.'

Jesus says to her, 'I AM, the one who is speaking to you.'[6]

---

1 This speech has suddenly taken on the magisterial voice of authority, very different from the weary one who said, 'Give me a drink (which, by the way, he never receives!).'

2 As in many languages, Greek has no separate word for 'husband' and 'man', or 'wife' and 'woman'. This command revives the 'sexual' or 'romantic' overtones of the conversation, only to dismiss them finally.

3 The woman is really entering into it now, and openly treats Jesus as authoritative, posing him a theological question about the appropriate place to worship. This in turn enables Jesus to deepen the revelation.

4 Spirit and Truth are two key ideas in John's Gospel; the woman and the reader alike are being drawn deeper into the mystery.

5 'Seeking' is a very important word in John's Gospel. See, for example, Jesus' first words after the Incarnation (1:38), and his first words after the Resurrection (20:15).

6 The climax of the woman's lesson in Christology. She has been a very apt pupil.

And at this, his disciples[1] turned up. And they were startled that he was talking to a Woman. However, no one said, 'What are you seeking' or 'Why are you talking to her?'[2]

So the woman left her bucket[3] and went off to the city and says to the people,[4] 'Come and see[5] a fellow who told me all the things I did. Do you think he might be the Messiah?' They went out of the city and went to him.

Meanwhile his disciples were asking him, saying, 'Rabbi, eat.' But he said to them, I have food that you do not know.' So the disciples said to each other, 'Could someone[6] have brought him something to eat?'

Jesus says to them, 'My food is that I should do the will of the one who sent me, and that I should complete his work. Don't you people say, "four months more and the harvest is coming"? Look, I tell you! Lift up your eyes and look at the farmlands; they are white for the harvest already! The one who reaps gets a reward and gathers fruit for eternal life, so that the sower may rejoice together with the reaper. For on this point the word is true, that the sower is one person and the reaper another. I sent you to reap where you had not laboured;[7] others have laboured, and you have entered into their labour.'

From that city, many of the Samaritans came to faith in him because of the word of the woman, who had testified, 'He told me everything I did.' So when the Samaritans came to him, they

---

1 They arrive at the wrong moment, and, as we shall see, only open their mouths to put their collective foot in it.

2 The evangelist is clearly very disapproving of their untutored reaction to the situation.

3 A very important moment: neither she nor Jesus has had the drink they were looking for, but he has given her something rather better. Now she symbolically leaves her old way of life and becomes an apostle.

4 This fearless evangelisation marks quite a change for the one who was only prepared to come to the well at a time when no one else would be there.

5 We recall Jesus' next words in the Gospel: 1:39.

6 They mean 'That Woman', of course, pursing their lips in disapproval. Johannine irony, or what?

7 This word appears three times in this sentence, and it is from the same root as the word for Jesus' exhaustion back at the beginning of the story. Both Jesus and the woman are way ahead of the disciples at this point.

asked him to remain with them; and he remained there for two days. And many more believed because of his word; and they said to the woman, 'No longer is it because of your gossip that we believe, for we have heard, and we know[1] that this is truly the Saviour[2] of the World.

Very often we have to grow slowly in our awareness of our own prejudices. In particular, we may have to learn to overrule our instinctive denial that there is any racism within us. This was something that I had to learn, slowly and painfully, in South Africa. In the next story, did Jesus have to learn the same lesson? Decide for yourself.

The Canaanite woman (Matthew 15:21-28)

Jesus went out from there, and went up to the regions of Tyre and Sidon. And look! A Canaanite woman from those parts came out and roared, 'Have mercy on me, Master, Son of David! My daughter is in a bad way with demons.'

But he didn't answer her a word. And his disciples came and kept on asking him, 'Send her packing, because she is roaring after us.' He answered, 'I was only sent to the lost sheep of the house of Israel.'

She, however, came and worshipped him, saying, 'Master, help me.' He answered, 'It is not good to take the children's bread and throw it to dogs.'

She said, 'Yes, Master – but you see, even dogs eat of the crumbs that fall from the table of their masters.'

. . . Then Jesus answered, 'O woman: great is your faith. Let it be done to you as you wish.'

And her daughter was healed at that moment.

---

1 Another very important idea in the Gospel of John.

2 They have reached a high point of revelation, thanks to the woman.

Who is the hero of this story? Quite clearly, the woman. The sole interest of the disciples is in getting rid of an embarrassment. Jesus confirms this by explaining to them that his mission is for 'Israelites only'; but she has the initiative to force the pace, and to compel Jesus to pay attention to 'a mere foreigner'. Her witty remark (twice using the word 'Master', which has already appeared twice earlier in the story) makes him stop and reflect, as I have tried to indicate by signalling a pregnant pause in the narrative. It should do the same for us.

The next passage also has to do with our thirst to reconnect with human beings. In the view of many scholars, one of the reasons that Christianity spread so rapidly was its emphasis on being open to all who accepted Jesus as 'Lord' or 'Messiah'. So they realised that the boundaries which, all too readily, we humans use to bolster our insecurities and to hide from people whom we see as 'threat' simply do not matter. In this passage, from his most ill-tempered letter, Paul is reminding his Galatians of the effects of baptism. This passage is about what the waters of baptism do. Paul is arguing against those who (to his fury) allowed themselves to be persuaded to retreat from the gospel he had preached to them. They were prepared to consider that in order to be a Christian it was necessary also to be an observant Jew. Paul insists on the freedom that God has given in Christ.

No artificial divisions in Christ (Galatians 3:26-29)

> For you are all children of God through faith in Christ Jesus.[1] For those of you who were baptised in Christ have put on Christ.[2]

---

1 This is Paul's particular contribution to the message.

2 This is a powerful metaphor, taken from the task of Greek actors who would put on the mask and cumbersome costume of someone like Agamemnon, and would actually become that person, while remaining himself or herself. If we can do that with Christ, then we shall find our thirst being slaked, and we shall be able to reach out to others, across boundaries.

In Christ there is neither Jew nor Greek [no racial divisions], nor slave nor free [no social divisions], no male and female [no distinctions of gender]. For all of you are one in Christ Jesus; and if you belong to Christ, then you are descended from Abraham, heirs according to God's promise.

Conclusion

Whether we recognise it or not, God invites us to reach out across the artificial boundaries we have constructed for ourselves out of fearfulness; and in our best moods we thirst to do so. The world into which Christianity first emerged was a very divided one, and part of the appeal of Christianity was that 'anyone can join'. Our world is similarly divided, and urgently needs the message that 'everyone belongs'.

Three questions
- Have you known this 'thirst to reach out across boundaries'?
- Have you experienced some of the difficulties of reaching out to other groups?
- Have you had any instructive failures in reaching out?

Closing Prayer

God, Creator of us all,
grant that we may never hide behind the artificial divisions
which our insecurities build into defences.
May we ever love all your creation
and reach out to all your human race. Amen.

CHAPTER 7

Thirsting for Life and Love

Opening Prayer

God Our Father,
help us to find you even when there is darkness and pain;
teach us to help others to find you when they need you;
bring us all in love to your Kingdom. Amen.

The Easter Mystery

We thirst for love. That is to say, we long to be loved, and to give ourselves in love. We have to be careful, however, for all too easily, without our noticing it, love can slip over into its parody. 'Love, love me do,' sang the Beatles in my youth, 'you know I'll love you' – but too often this can be translated as 'Jump into bed with me – because I want to jump into bed with you', which has a link with love, but which can also be a ghastly travesty of it. Sex, like its near relatives Money and Power, can be a marvellous thing, but if love, real love, ceases to control it, then things go wrong. Or, to put it another way, if we are determined to keep God out of it, it will all end in tears.

So it has to be real love. But how do I know that my love is real? A useful rule of thumb is that real love will tend to be costly, to make me less selfish and more generous, to lead me to give first place to serving the beloved. Another useful rule of thumb is that real love always has something of the Easter mystery about it, of life out of death, of Resurrection after the Cross.

Perhaps this is only another way of saying the same thing. For the Jesus story is the story of what love looks like when you live it out from birth to death. And the Christian claim is that love is never defeated; people can do their worst (they did to Jesus on that terrible Good Friday), but their worst is simply not good enough to defeat the power of love. If you are using this book as a way of praying through Lent, then you will have reached this chapter just as the Church turns to the high drama of Holy Week; but even if you have not, the 'Easter mystery' of death and resurrection is the climax of the Christian journey, and it is fitting to end with it, to remind us what love really means.

Love and resurrection life: the same thing (1 John 4:7-16)

Beloved, let us love each other; because love is from God. And everyone who loves is born of God, and knows God. The one who doesn't love doesn't know God – because God is love.

This is how God's love was revealed in us – God sent his only-begotten Son into the world, so that we might live through him. This is what love consists in: it's not that we have loved God. Instead, it's that God loved us, and sent his Son as the expiation for our sins.

Beloved – if that's how God loved us, we have a duty to love each other. No one has ever seen God. If we love each other, God remains in us, and God's love is made perfect in us.

This is how we know that we remain in God and God in us, that he has given us his Spirit.

And we have seen, and we bear witness, that the Father has sent his Son as Saviour of the World. Anyone who admits that Jesus is the Son of God, God remains in that person, and that person in God.

And we have known and have come to faith in the love which God has in us.

Three Easter moments

Let me share three Easter moments which I have lived through in South Africa over twelve years or so. The first was 11 February 1990, when Nelson Mandela was released from prison after twenty-seven years. It was an extraordinary moment, not least for the message that he brought out of prison with him, of reconciliation in a world of bitterness. Its effect was made all the sharper by the incompetence on that day of the South African Broadcasting Corporation, at that time something of a lapdog of the apartheid government: they produced footage about him, obviously intended as his obituary should he die in prison, which demonised him as a communist agitator. It simply served to underline the laughable ineptitude of the forces of evil.

The second was on 4 May 1994, when Mandela was inaugurated as President. There were several who gulped with emotion to see the Generals of the South African Defence Force saluting their old enemy as he mounted the platform. And there was the unforgettable moment when the crowd heard the sound of approaching fighter planes and instinctively ducked, before realising 'they're ours!' – it was a flyover, with the planes streaming the colours of the new South African flag, and not (as it might have been) an attempted coup.

The third was in 1995, at the final of the Rugby World Cup, when Mandela won the hearts of many white South Africans who had been his sworn enemies. No one who saw it will ever forget the sight of the old man wearing the Springbok shirt, and jiving with the team's captain, the impeccably Afrikaans Francois Pienaar.

Moments such as these do more than a thousand sermons to signal that there is always hope that good will gain the victory over evil. That is what we thirst for, even in our deepest grief.

Jesus' terrible last words (Mark 15:34)

Christians run the dreadful risk of giving glib answers to suffering people who are thirsting for meaning. Glib answers do not do the trick, and are an impertinence. While it is our conviction that even in the worst catastrophes God is at work, making things better and supplying the meaning for which we thirst, we have, however, to take seriously the meaninglessness and pain which people, including ourselves at times, experience.

> And at the ninth hour, Jesus shouted in a mighty voice,
> 'Eloi, Eloi, lema sabachthani?', which if you translate it
> means: 'My God, my God, why have you forsaken me?'

Some people die an apparently meaningless death; and both they and we thirst to find meaning in it. Only in God can we find it. Some readers of this text point out that Jesus' words are the opening of Psalm 22, which ends with a great cry of confidence in God. So, they argue, Jesus is not giving in to despair, but is in fact proclaiming his faith. Perhaps. But the fact is that Mark quotes Jesus, not in the Hebrew in which he would ordinarily have recited the psalm, but in Jesus' native tongue, Aramaic. So it seems that Mark intends us to see these as Jesus' dying words. We do, however, notice that they are addressed to God, no matter how absent that God may seem to be. Only God can slake our thirst, even a God that seems impossibly remote.

Blinded by tears (John 20:11-18)

Our next story is an extraordinary one of how grief is consoled, without being belittled, in the dispensation of God.

> Meanwhile, Mary [Magdalene] stood near the tomb, outside, weeping. So while she was weeping, she stooped down into the tomb. And she sees two angels, sitting in white [clothes], one by

the head and one by the feet,[1] where the body of Jesus had lain.[2] And they say to her, 'Woman, why are you weeping?'[3]

She says to them, 'They have taken my Lord, and I do not know where they have put him.'[4] As she said this, she turned backwards and saw Jesus standing there. And she did not know that it was Jesus. Jesus says to her, 'Woman, why are you weeping? Whom are you looking for?'[5]

[Mary], thinking he was the gardener,[6] says to him, 'Lord,[7] if you have taken him away, tell me where you have put him, and I shall remove him.'

Jesus says to her, 'Mary.' Turning round, she says to him in Aramaic, 'Rabbouni[8] (translated as teacher).'

Jesus says to her, 'Don't touch me, for I have not yet gone up to the Father. But go to my brethren and say to them, 'I am going up to my Father and your Father, both my God and your God.'[9]

Mary Magdalene comes announcing to the disciples, 'I have seen the Lord', and that he had said these things to her.

This is a beautiful encounter, and a demonstration of how the Easter mystery works; it comes to us in the midst of our grief, for that is where our love reveals itself most powerfully. It is also where the love of God for us is most powerfully revealed, though we cannot always see it that way.

1 The reader is bound to ask, 'Whose head and whose feet?'
2 Or 'was lying'.
3 Jesus will shortly ask her the same question.
4 Mary is very nearly there: she is able to call Jesus 'Lord', and she knows very well that she cannot live without him. He is the one she is thirsting for.
5 Once again we are reminded of the arrest in the garden: John 18:4, 7. And remember 1:38. It is a good question always to put to our thirsty selves, and to others who are thirsty.
6 So her Christology was not at this stage all that advanced!
7 She is not far off the truth at this stage, for she addresses him as 'Lord'; in one sense it is perfectly adequate for a passing gardener; in another sense it is absolutely right for Jesus.
8 This exchange of recognition is a beautiful moment.
9 All that she was thirsting for is now given her, in the context of the only reality that matters: that God is, and that God cares.

Our last text makes this point about the Easter mystery in a rather different way.

Jesus on real love – the night before he died: (John 13:34-35, 14:28, 15:12-17)

It is worth recalling at this point that Jesus utters these words not very many verses after he has shown the meaning of love by washing the disciples' feet, and very soon after Judas Iscariot has gone out into the night. Real love is at its best when things are at their very worst.

> 'I give you all a new commandment, that you love each other as I have loved you, so that you also may love each other. By this everyone will know that you are my disciples, if you have love among each other . . .'

> 'If you loved me, you would rejoice that I am going to the Father, for the Father is greater than I am . . .'[1]

> 'This is my command, that you love each other as I have loved you. No one has greater love than this, that a person lay down their life on behalf of their friends.[2] You are my friends, if you do what I command you. I no longer call you servants,[3] because the servant does not know what their Lord is doing. But I have called you friends; because everything that I have heard from my Father I have made known to you. You did not choose me – no, I chose you. And I put you in place, that you should go and bear fruit[4] and your fruit should remain . . . this I command you all, that you love each other.'

✿ 1 We boggle at the thought of rejoicing in the absence of the Beloved – but it does happen.
2 Real love, that is to say, is *costly*.
3 Or 'slaves'.
4 Love is not just a cosy 'feel-good' phenomenon; it has its effect on others.

The world in which we live thirsts, cries out, for love such as this; a love that is the real thing, putting others' needs above our own, and finding joy in doing so. This generous quality is what distinguishes it from either lust or sentimentality, both of which can masquerade as love unless we are alert to the danger.

Three questions
- What has been your experience of inexplicable suffering? Were you able to find any meaning in it?
- Have you ever known examples of 'real love'? What impact did they make on you?
- How were they different from either 'lust' or 'sentimentality'?

Closing Prayer

This prayer of St Ignatius Loyola comes at the end of his 'Contemplation for Obtaining Love', with which he concludes the *Spiritual Exercises*. Pray it thoughtfully.

Take, Lord, and receive

all my freedom,
all my memory,
all my understanding
and my entire will;
all my property and possessions.

It was you, Lord, who gave it to me.
To you, Lord, I hand it back.
All is yours – make your arrangements entirely at your pleasure.
Give me the love of you, and your grace,
which is enough for me. Amen.